FROM MAO TOWARD MODERNITY: THE INCREASING WESTERNIZATION OF THE PEOPLE'S LIBERATION ARMY

ABSTRACT

FROM MAO TOWARD MODERNITY: THE INCREASING WESTERNIZATION OF THE PEOPLE'S LIBERATION ARMY, by MAJ Christopher J. Kelshaw, 63 pages.

While the People's Republic of China (PRC) continues to grow as a great power within the Asian region, its military continues to seek and develop commensurate military capabilities. People's Liberation Army (PLA) ambitions to modernize provoke a number of questions regarding underlying PLA rationale and motivation. Specifically, what has driven the PLA to choose to become less of a rural based guerilla force primarily focused on defense, and more of a modern, and Western-like standing military with a credible offensive capability? Further, what events, in particular, have shaped, and continue to shape PLA thinking in this regard? This monograph argues that three events in particular—the 1979 Sino-Vietnamese conflict, the 1991 United States (U.S.) Gulf War, and U.S. and North Atlantic Treaty Organization (NATO) military action against the Federal Republic of Yugoslavia in 1999—have contributed to a consistent PLA movement toward greater Westernization in its approaches toward and preparations for war. The abysmal performance of the PLA during the 1979 Sino-Vietnamese conflict marked the nadir for the Maoist operating concept of people's war, and served as a point of departure toward greater military Westernization. Additionally, both the 1991 Gulf War, and U.S. and NATO military action in Kosovo served to reinforce the trend in modern Chinese military development toward greater Westernization.

ACKNOWLEDGMENTS

I would like to thank Dr. Michael Mihalka for his guidance throughout the process that led to this monograph. Most importantly, I would like to give special thanks to my wife, Iris, for her unending patience and support.

TABLE OF CONTENTS

ACRONYMS vi

TABLES vii

INTRODUCTION 1

    Definitions... 4

LITERATURE REVIEW 4

METHODOLOGY AND ORGANIZATION 15

CASE STUDIES 18

    The 1979 Sino-Vietnamese Conflict.. 19
    The 1990-1991 Gulf War... 30
    U.S. and NATO Military Action against the Republic of Yugoslavia.................... 37
    PLA Westernization and the Regional Balance of Power....................................... 47

CONCLUSION 50

BIBLIOGRAPHY 52

ACRONYMS

CCP	Chinese Communist Part
CMC	Central Military Commission
FRY	Federal Republic of Yugoslavia
GDP	Gross Domestic Product
NATO	North Atlantic Treaty Organization
PLA	People's Liberation Army
PRC	People's Republic of China

TABLES

Page

Table 1. Western Characteristics of Warfare across Three Case Studies 18

Table 2. Manifestation of Western Characteristics of Warfare Post-Sino-Vietnamese
Conflict 29

Table 3. Manifestation of Western Characteristics of Warfare Post-U.S.-led 1990-1991
Gulf War against Iraq 37

Table 4. Manifestation of Western Characteristics of Warfare and Post-U.S./NATO
Operations against FRY 47

Table 5. Western Characteristics of Warfare across Three Case Studies 51

INTRODUCTION

While the People's Republic of China (PRC) continues to grow as a great power within

the Asian region, its military continues to seek and develop commensurate military capabilities.[1]

As a result, the Chinese People's Liberation Army (PLA), which began in 1927 as the Chinese

Red Army of Workers, has moved well past its rural based revolutionary guerilla force roots, and

more toward what is a comparatively more modern military force.

Today, the PLA, which now includes both a People's Liberation Army Air Force and a

People's Liberation Army Navy, continues to face increasing pressure to modernize its force

capabilities.[2] This involves not only focusing on the simple defense of the Chinese mainland, but

also on protecting the ever-expanding sovereign interests of the PRC.[3]

While the pace of this military modernization has certainly fluctuated over the past 30

years due to internal and external factors, it appears that the PLA has been relatively consistent in

its efforts to gain and integrate means and methods similar to Western militaries into its

approaches to war fighting.[4]

---

[1]Great power, as used here, describes a state with a level of diplomatic, economic, social, and military power that affords it significant influence over other states who must consider it when undertaking any action or policy within a given region. See Paul Gordon Lauren, Gordon Alexander Craig, and Alexander L. George, *Force and Statecraft: Diplomatic Challenges of Our Time*, 4th ed. (New York, NY: Oxford University Press, 2007), 8, 19-21, 34, 40, 181.

[2]Roy Kamphausen, David Lai, and Andrew Scobell, *The PLA at Home and Abroad: Assessing the Operational Capabilities of China's Military*, eds. Roy Kamphausen, David Lai, and Andrew Scobell (Carlisle, PA: Strategic Studies Institute, U.S. Army War College, 2010), 9, 12.

[3]For example, the PRC has been a major participant in both United Nations humanitarian relief efforts (e.g., Haiti in 2010), and continues to participate in multilateral anti-piracy missions off the coast of eastern Africa.

[4]Mao Zedong's economic Great Leap Forward (1958-1960) and the subsequent Cultural Revolution (1966-1976) inspired by him served to stymie many real efforts to modernize during these particularly tumultuous periods within China. Additionally, the Chinese Communist Party's policy choice to subordinate military modernization in favor of first modernizing PRC

If so, then it is this ambition to modernize, and perhaps move away from its more foundational operating concepts, that provokes a number of questions regarding underlying PLA rationale and motivation. Specifically, what has driven the PLA to choose to become less a rural based guerilla force primarily focused on defense, and more of a modern, and Western-like standing military with a credible offensive capability? Further, what events, in particular, have shaped, and continue to shape PLA thinking in this regard?

This monograph offers answers to these particular questions. Specifically, it argues that three events in particular—the 1979 Sino-Vietnamese conflict, the 1991 United States (U.S.) Gulf War, and U.S. and NATO military actions against the Republic of Yugoslavia in 1999—have significantly shaped PLA thinking, and have been the primary and most proximate impetus behind PLA movement toward greater Westernization.

The abysmal performance of the PLA during the 1979 Sino-Vietnamese conflict marked the nadir for the Maoist operating concept of people's war, and served as a point of departure toward greater military Westernization. Additionally, the 1991 Gulf War, and the 1999 U.S.-led NATO military intervention to prevent Serbian aggression against Muslims and Albanian Kosovars both served to reinforce this trend. Furthermore, these cases relate to Chinese Communist Party (CCP) concerns over its ability to defend and protect PRC sovereignty, given China's history with direct Western impositions against that sovereignty in the past.

During the 19th century both Britain and France, along with other Western states, were able to impose mercantilist designs upon a reluctant pre-modern Chinese Qing state primarily due to the latter's military weakness.[5] When considering China's military development, this is a

---

agricultural, industrial, and technological developments beginning in the early 1980s also served to limit modernization efforts during this period.

[5]Rhoads Murphey, *East Asia: A New History*, 5th ed. (Boston, MA: Longman, 2010), 285-304.

particularly important historical point that provides much-needed context for understanding PRC modernization in general, and PLA military modernization in particular.

As a result, China's political leaders remain well aware that the PRC must continue efforts to develop the sufficient military means to protect its sovereign interests in order to rectify what many consider to be China's century of humiliation.[6] For many Chinese, a PRC without a modern military capability is essentially an incomplete great power that risks having its sovereignty imposed upon as before. Issues like those regarding Taiwanese independence, or contested areas within the South China Sea are just two highly relevant examples that could likely draw in more cutting edge militaries, or their allies (e.g., the U.S. and Japan).[7]

That said, while many of the events that have occurred in both pre-modern and modern Chinese history continue to inform Chinese political and military culture today, this monograph limits its scope to events that have measurably influenced the PLA during the latter part of the 20th century. This is primarily due to their particular proximity to certain aspects of China's sovereign interests. By doing so, this monograph deals primarily with and hopes to contribute to the vast and ongoing discussion regarding China's actual military evolution, while offsetting other interpretations that may overemphasize those more mystical or esoteric aspects of pre-modern Chinese war fighting.[8]

---

[6]Information Office of the State Council, The People's Republic of China, "China's National Defense," China.org.cn, July 1998, http://www.china.org.cn/e-white/5/index.htm (accessed 5 February 2014), 15.

[7]U.S. Department of Defense (DOD), *Annual Report to Congress: Military and Security Developments Involving the People's Republic of China 2013,* U.S. Department of Defense, 2013, http://www.defense.gov/pubs/2013_china_report_final.pdf (accessed 22 February 2014), 3-5.

[8]Timothy L. Thomas, *Dragon Bytes : Chinese Information-War Theory and Practice from 1995-2003* (Fort Leavenworth, KS: Foreign Military Studies Office, 2004); and Timothy L. Thomas, *Decoding the Virtual Dragon* (Fort Leavenworth, KS: Foreign Military Studies Office, 2007).

This monograph begins with a discussion of the relevant literature from both a Western and Chinese perspective on PLA westernization. The second section briefly discusses a methodological approach. The third section explores three case studies—PLA operations and performance during the 1979 Sino-Vietnamese conflict, as well as PLA attitudes and actions following both the U.S. led Gulf War in 1990-1991, and the U.S.-led NATO military intervention in Kosovo in 1999. The fourth section moves beyond these cases to discuss other factors related to PLA Westernization to include how the PLA hopes to benefit from its modernization efforts along Western lines in relation to its security objectives and the constraints it faces.

Definitions

The term Westernization is central to the discussion here, and means to convey the process of PLA military modernization efforts or actions that are similar to, or influenced by the military characteristics, cultures, and systems endemic to the armies of Europe or North America (i.e., the U.S.).

LITERATURE REVIEW

When considering the evolutionary development of the PLA, it is prudent to consult both Western and non-Western perspectives. Limiting an inquiry such as this to just one perspective, either Chinese or non-Chinese, would certainly be incomplete. More importantly, a less than comprehensive approach would run the risk of mirror imaging (i.e., analyzing the PLA and understanding it solely through Western eyes).

Therefore, a number of Western and Chinese official and unofficial sources have been useful in determining both the characteristics of a Western style of warfare, as well as the nature and motivations behind the evolution of the PLA. Beginning with the former, there are a number of sources that are particularly helpful in pinning down what constitutes a traditional and distinctly Western war fighting archetype.

4

Victor David Hanson's *The Western Way of War: Infantry Battle in Classical Greece* provides an historical perspective from which to view warfare's development in the West through the ages. As the title suggests, Hanson sees these Western war fighting characteristics as originating in classical Greece, and that this approach has traditionally sought an "unequivocal and instantaneous result" gained primarily by "firepower and heavy defensive armament."[9] Additionally, Hanson argues that a distinctly Western way of war is characterized by seeking the "decisive battle" in an "all or nothing" military engagement.[10]

In Hanson's telling, the overall military goal in Western warfare has been to create ". . . the absolute destruction of the enemy's armed forces in the field," while seeking to "end the fighting quickly and efficiently."[11] Hanson argues that these particular Western military attitudes and relatively brutal approaches to warfare have "baffled and terrified our adversaries from the non-Western world for more than 2,500 years . . ."[12] He further states, "outnumbered Western commanders have never been dismayed by the opportunity to achieve an incredible victory [by relying heavily on] the use of superior weapons, tactics, and cohesion among men."[13] Although contentious, Hansen's work does support the idea of Western proclivity for a form of warfare that is characterized by battles that are decisive, quick, and intense in terms of firepower.

The *Cambridge Illustrated History of Warfare: The Triumph of the West* edited by Geoffrey Parker is an authoritative work that provides five very useful and simple characteristics that help define what can be considered a Western style and approach to waging war across

---

[9]Victor Davis Hanson, *The Western Way of War: Infantry Battle in Classical Greece* (New York, NY: Knopf, 1989), xii, 9.

[10]Ibid., xii.

[11]Ibid., 9, 13.

[12]Ibid., 9.

[13]Ibid., 15.

time.[14] The first of these includes the observation that Western militaries "have always placed heavy reliance on superior technology, usually to compensate for inferior numbers."[15] In other words, military quality seems to have been a reasonable alternative to quality if the latter was sufficiently unavailable or unaffordable. This is particularly appropriate to the subject of PLA Westernization given the recent move by the Chinese military to reduce force numbers in favor of increasing the quality of both humans and hardware.

Secondly, from the ancient Greeks to the "rise of missile weapons," a Western way of warfare "has always exalted discipline [through professional training] . . . as the primary instrument that turns bands of men fighting as individuals into soldiers fighting as part of organized units," whether on land or sea.[16] Third, and quite similar to Hanson, is "a [Western] vision of war centered on winning a decisive victory that [brings] about the enemy's unconditional surrender."[17] Napoleonic warfare waged during the 19th century, unlike its 18th century European equivalent, supports this assertion given the former's reliance on large conscripted armies that sought actual combat through mass and concentrated attack, as opposed to the latter's more risk and casualty averse variant. Additionally, while Parker points out that both the Chinese and Japanese ancient military traditions "also placed a high premium on technology and discipline," his last two Western military characteristics—a relatively "unique ability to change as well as to conserve . . . military practices as need arose [along with the] power to

---

[14]Geoffrey Parker, *The Cambridge Illustrated History of Warfare: The Triumph of the West*, rev. and updated ed. (Cambridge, NY: Cambridge University Press, 2008).

[15]Ibid., 2.

[16]Ibid., 3.

[17]Ibid., 5.

finance those changes"—are critical distinctions when comparing Western and non-Western ways of war fighting.[18]

However, neither Hanson nor Parker includes another characteristic—casualty aversion—that can add to an ever-evolving Western style of warfare.[19] Specifically, some have argued that because of an increasing reliance on technology in war fighting, Western policy makers seek "virtually bloodless interventions" that mirror "the casualty-avoiding methods of eighteenth-century warfare."[20] This no doubt presents an appealing option for political leaders in relatively more open and pluralistic societies that seek to build consensus for military action, while simultaneously appeasing their constituents who vibrantly oppose such measures. Even so, while this particular characteristic is somewhat suspect it is interesting to ponder the level of tolerance on the part of China's leadership and its people for sustaining large numbers of casualties in a conflict with an opponent that is relatively more casualty averse.[21] Furthermore, it seems possible that if a high tolerance exists, it may provide an increasingly Westernized PLA with an additional military advantage.

Taken together, Hanson, Parker, and the relatively recent notion of casualty aversion, all support a particular conception of a Western military approach to warfare. Key characteristics include a continuous adaptation of military methods and approaches, a preference for high quality, professional, and technologically superior hard power military means, the necessary allocation of sufficient fiscal resources in order to acquire these means and methods, and a goal of

---

[18]Parker, 5.

[19]Edward N. Luttwak, "Toward Post-Heroic Warfare," *Foreign Affairs* 74, no. 3 (1995): 109-123.

[20]Ibid.

[21]Michael P. Noonan, "The Illusion of Bloodless Victories," *Orbis* 41, no. 2 (1997): 308-320.

utterly destroying a sometimes numerically superior adversary's will to resist with minimal cost in terms of manpower lost. Most importantly, these characteristics, along with the more recent ideas of casualty aversion, can serve as clear criteria that can be applied to relevant cases involving PLA actions, observations, and attitudes in order to illustrate increasing Westernization.

When considering the Sino-Vietnamese case and its relationship as a starting point for greater PLA Westernization, Gerald Segal's *Defending China* provides an excellent account of that conflict, along with other important events that have shaped China's security and foreign policies. Segal includes clear descriptions of PRC and PLA goals and objectives tied to Chinese military actions against a relatively more proficient Vietnamese military in 1979, and how the PLA was ultimately unable to achieve these because of its low level of military effectiveness.

Specifically, and quite clearly, Segal asserts ". . . the 1979 Sino-Vietnamese war was China's most important foreign policy failure since 1949, and [that] the main reason for this failure was the poor performance of the PLA."[22] Additionally, Segal shows how the PLA had failed to modernize sufficiently during the 1950s and 1960s, while remaining overly reliant upon a purely defensive operating concept (i.e., people's war) that lacked utility in a purely offensive and more modern context.

Supporting Segal's assertions is *Chinese Warfighting: The PLA Experience since 1949* by Mark Ryan, David Finkelstein, and Michael McDevitt's. Ryan, Finklestein, and McDevitt provide an analysis of the Sino-Vietnamese conflict, but do so by incorporating the Vietnamese perspective. These authors shed additional light on the low level of PLA capability at a time when "the [Chinese military] had been ravaged by the dislocations of the Cultural Revolution, had not engaged in combat for ten years, and had not yet modernized its forces . . ."[23] Those Vietnamese

---

[22]Gerald Segal, *Defending China* (Oxford, NY: Oxford University Press, 1985), 211.

[23]Mark A. Ryan, David Michael Finkelstein, and Michael A. McDevitt, *Chinese Warfighting: The PLA Experience since 1949* (Armonk, NY: M.E. Sharpe, 2003), 230.

8

that fought against the PLA viewed their Chinese opponents as "untrained and not combat effective . . . suffering enormous casualties" for relatively little gain.[24] Most importantly, Segal, Ryan, Finkelstein, and McDevitt support the assertion made here that these PLA military shortfalls and the resultant poor performance served as the impetus toward increased Westernization efforts that were to come.

David Shambaugh's *Modernizing China's Military: Progress, Problems, and Prospects* and Dennis Blasko's *The Chinese Army Today* (2006 and 2012), both particularly informative, and provide keen insight into the factors that have shaped PLA development over time.[25] Additionally, both authors are experienced China scholars and analysts whose assessments and conclusions regarding China's military development are highly reliant upon official Chinese primary sources. Furthermore, Shambaugh and Blasko provide well-researched insight into PLA thinking vis-à-vis the U.S. military's performance during the 1990-1991 Gulf War, and its strongly influential impact on the PLA. Both authors also agree that this particular case was a significant event that shaped the development of the PLA.

After the Gulf War had ended, both PRC and PLA officials viewed the overwhelming American military success as a threat to its one China policy regarding Taiwan, and feared how a similar U.S. led coalition could form to intervene in a dispute over Taiwanese independence with the U.S. Many PLA officials believed that if this were to occur, the PLA would not be able to protect PRC sovereign interests against a more Westernized military force.

As a result of witnessing the U.S. military's capabilities in action, Shambaugh states "the PLA's goal [became to] develop a multifaceted, technologically modern force structure capable

---

[24]Ryan et al., 230.

[25]Dennis J Blasko, *Chinese Army Today: Tradition and Transformation for the 21st Century* (New York, NY: Routledge, 2012), 288; and David Shambaugh, *Modernizing China's Military: Progress, Problems, and Prospects* (Berkeley, CA: University of California Press, 2002), 228.

of pursuing multiple missions in a regional context . . ."[26] According to Shambaugh and Blasko, the PLA thereafter oriented itself toward developing a more appropriate operating concept and the necessary means to carry it out in a local and limited conflict against a technologically superior foe.

A more recent book of value on China's military development is Larry Wortzel's *The Dragon Extends Its Reach: Chinese Military Power Goes Global*.[27] Wortzel, a retired U.S. Army officer with extensive professional and academic knowledge of China and its military, supports the idea that "as China's national interests [have] expanded significantly beyond its immediate borders, its military [has likewise expanded] its capabilities and scope of operations."[28] Additionally, Wortzel provides valuable information that contributes to the general view of a PLA that has become a more Westernized armed force that has "systematically, if slowly, modernized its equipment, focused on training its personnel, and changed its mission to meet the challenges of new times . . ."[29]

Since 2002, the U.S. Defense Department has been required by law to submit an annual report on military and security developments involving the PRC.[30] These official reports focus on PLA developments and operating concepts, as well as their implications for U.S. security. Most importantly, and when considered together, they help generally trace more recent PLA

---

[26]Shambaugh, *Modernizing China's Military: Progress, Problems, and Prospects,* 71.

[27]Larry M. Wortzel, *The Dragon Extends Its Reach: Chinese Military Power Goes Global*, 1st ed. (Sterling, VA: Potomac Books, 2013), 240.

[28]Ibid., x.

[29]Ibid.

[30]For the most recent report, see U.S. DOD, *Annual Report to Congress: Military and Security Developments Involving the People's Republic of China 2013,* 3.

developments, while providing evidence that supports the idea of a consistent PLA effort to military modernization along Western lines.

From time to time, certain prominent China watchers, such as James Mulvenon, Andrew N.D. Yang, and again, David Finkelstein, have written a number of reports on China's military modernization for prominent think tanks such as the RAND and Center for Naval Analysis corporations.[31] These reports are especially valuable given their access to and extensive research of many primary PLA source documents. Source materials like these strongly underscore the assertion that both the Gulf War and U.S.-led NATO intervention against the Republic of Yugoslavia in Kosovo particularly influence PLA modernization efforts.

For example, in their report *Seeking Truth from Facts: A Retrospective on Chinese Military Studies in the Post-Mao Era*, Mulvenon and Yang point out that, after the 1991 Persian Gulf War, the PLA experienced an unpleasant and clear realization that much of their equipment, weapons, personnel, organization, and training were sorely "antiquated" in relation to the U.S. military. This stark observation acutely elevated these matters to "a new and much higher level of significance" within the PRC government.[32]

As stated above, this monograph would severely lack a comprehensive perspective if it did not consider Chinese sources, in addition to those Western. That said, a number of these sources are particularly fundamental, and have profoundly shaped traditional PLA attitudes and approaches to war fighting.

---

[31]James C. Mulvenon and Andrew N.D. Yang, eds., *Seeking Truth from Facts : A Retrospective on Chinese Military Studies in the Post-Mao Era* (Santa Monica, CA: National Security Research Division, RAND, 2001), 213; and James C. Mulvenon and David Michael Finkelstein, *China's Revolution in Doctrinal Affairs Emerging Trends in the Operational Art of the Chinese People's Liberation Army*, CNA Corporation, 2005, http://www.cna.org/documents/ DoctrineBook.pdf (accessed 5 February 2014), 381.

[32]Mulvenon and Yang, 101.

Understanding the impact that Mao Zedong's own writings had on military matters is key to understanding early PLA operating concepts that have shaped Chinese approaches to war fighting throughout much of China's modern era.[33] Specifically important is Mao's concept of people's war, which has strongly shaped PLA approaches to Chinese war fighting up to the 1980s.[34]

The central concept of Maoist military thought and people's war was that of "man over weapons."[35] Mao believed that the outcome of any armed conflict was "ultimately determined by the 'human factor'—popularly mobilized and politically motivated soldiers, fighting in accordance with the correct strategy and tactics."[36] For example, in December 1929, during the Ninth CCP Congress of the Red Fourth Army, Mao warned of "non-proletarian ideas" within the army that were "hinder[ing] the application of the Party's correct line."[37] Mao was specifically targeting what he considered the emergence of a "purely military viewpoint" that neglected political matters, which he considered to have primacy over purely military matters like training.[38] Consequently, Mao sought to increase the amount of political training for those within the army at the expense of military professionalism.

Throughout much of the 20th century, Mao stressed the need for the PLA to adopt people's war because of China's relatively weak position, particularly concerning the

---

[33]Mao Zedong, *Selected Military Writings of Mao Tse-Tung*, ed. Combat Studies Institute, (Fort Leavenworth, KS: U.S. Army Command and General Staff College, 2012), 285.

[34]Ellis Joffe, *The Chinese Army after Mao* (Cambridge, MA: Harvard University Press, 1987), 1-23.

[35]Ibid., 73.

[36]Ibid.

[37]Zedong, 53.

[38]Ibid., 53-56.

Kuomintang nationalists, the Japanese, the Soviet Union, and the U.S.[39] In order to compensate for this weakness, the PLA would place heavy emphasis on political and ideological needs ahead of practical military considerations. The result was that by the late 1970s, there was a "sharp decline in the professional standards of the PLA."[40]

However, more recent official PRC and PLA documents and writings provide valuable insight into the thinking and policies behind PLA modernization post-Mao, particularly throughout the 1980s, 1990s, and 2000s. For example, PLA officials frequently wrote articles in influential party papers, such as *Jiefangjun Bao* (i.e., *Liberation Army Daily*, or *PLA Daily*) in order to argue for a particular policy or approach. While this practice continues today, those writings at the time were particularly important in that they supported the idea behind increasing PLA modernization from the 1980s onward.[41]

Chinese government statements regarding military policies, and operating concepts, also serve as a good starting point for a more relevant analysis. For example, official pronouncements and speeches, like one given by Deng Xiaoping in 1985 to the Central Military Commission (CMC), provide evidence of official CCP recognition for the need to modernize across all aspects of Chinese society, especially militarily.

Sources like these help reveal that during the latter part of the 20th century, and after Mao's death in 1976, China's leaders assessed that a major conflict between the Soviet Union and the U.S. was unlikely, and that China's decision to open its economy to foreign trade and investment was sound because of this now improved security environment. This attitude, along

---

[39]Zedong, 53-56.

[40]Joffe, 74.

[41]Liu Huaqing, "Unswervingly Advance Along the Road of Building a Modern Army with Chinese Characteristics," *Jiefangjun Bao* (18 August 1993): 15-22, Foreign Broadcast Information Service.

with the recognition that the PLA performed poorly during the Sino-Vietnamese conflict, motivated CCP officials like Deng to claim that China could now "concentrate without fear on the drive for [military] modernization," and that the PLA was now required to make every effort to "absorb as many useful things as possible from other countries."[42] Official party statements like these support the claim made here that military modernization along Western-lines became official policy in the wake of the 1979 Sino-Vietnamese conflict.

In the aftermath of the 1991 Gulf War, PLA white papers placed even greater emphasis on the urgent need to increase military modernization efforts to effectively counter military forces that were seen as vastly superior. In a 1998 white paper, the PLA stated, "military forces still occupy an important position in state security," and recognized that the "military advantages" of other countries (i.e., the U.S.) "pose military threats" to PRC security.[43] More recently, the PLA's 2010 white paper entitled "China's National Defense in 2010" stated that its continued goal is to ". . . build a fortified national defense and strong armed forces compatible with national security and development interests [and that such efforts are] a strategic task of China's modernization . . ."[44]

The PLA's most recent white paper, entitled "The Diversified Employment of China's Armed Forces," published in April 2013, is quite clear regarding the PLA's desire to modernize its forces along Western lines in order to counter threats to its sovereign interests. It states:

---

[42]Xiaoping Deng and Zhongguo gong chan dang. Zhong yang Makesi En'gesi Liening Sidalin zhu zuo bian yi ju., *Selected Works of Deng Xiaoping, 1982-1992.* vol. 3, 1st ed. (Beijing, China: Foreign Languages Press, 1994), 133.

[43]Information Office of the State Council, The People's Republic of China, "China's National Defense," 1998, 13.

[44]Information Office of the State Council, The People's Republic of China, "China's National Defense in 2010," Xinuanet, 31 March 2011, http://news.xinhuanet.com/english2010/china/2011-03/31/c_13806851.htm (accessed 12 November 2013).

. . . it is a strategic task of China's modernization drive as well as a strong guarantee for China's peaceful development to build a strong national defense and powerful armed forces which are commensurate with China's international standing and meet the needs of its security and development interests. China's armed forces act to meet the new requirements of China's national development and security strategies, follow the theoretical guidance of the Scientific Outlook on Development, speed up the transformation of the generating mode of combat effectiveness, *build a system of modern military forces with Chinese characteristics, enhance military strategic guidance and diversify the ways of employing armed forces as the times require*. China's armed forces provide a security guarantee and strategic support for national development, and make due contributions to the maintenance of world peace and regional stability [emphasis author].[45]

In summary, much of the official and non-official Chinese and Western sources available seem to heavily support the idea that the PLA is modernizing along Western lines, and that it is adopting both methods and means that are commonly associated with the militaries of Western or Western-like states, such as the U.S. and Japan. Additionally, the available literature, some discussed above, highlights the 1979 Sino-Vietnamese conflict, the 1991 Gulf War, and the 1999 U.S.-led NATO military intervention against the Republic of Yugoslavia as being particularly important in driving modern Westernization trends within the Chinese military.

METHODOLOGY AND ORGANIZATION

As shown in the above review of relevant literature, this monograph consults both Western and Chinese primary and secondary sources that provide historical evidence and expert analysis to support those arguments made here. Additionaly, this monograph relies primarily on the qualitative analysis of a particular set of historic cases.

To be sure, any exploration of PLA efforts to modernize throughout its history would benefit from the inclusion of a much larger and more comprehensive number of cases that would extend from its early 20th century origins up to the present day. However, such an all-inclusive

---

[45]Information Office of the State Council, The People's Republic of China, "The Diversified Employment of China's Armed Forces," Xinhuanet, 16 April 2013, http://news.xinhuanet.com/english/china/2013-04/16/c_132312681.htm (accessed 13 November 2013).

approach is beyond the scope of this monograph. That said, three significant cases have been chosen in order to provide a better and more contemporary understanding of PLA Westernization efforts.

The first case considered is China's punitive cross-border conflict with Vietnam in 1979, and the after effects of that event. The second case chosen will examine PLA actions and initiatives that followed the U.S. military's Operation Desert Storm from 1990-1991 in order to illustrate increased efforts by the PLA to westernize in the wake of that conflict. The third and final historic case will likewise encompass what have been the PLA's views, opinions, and resultant actions that emerged both during and after the U.S.-led NATO air campaign against Serbian President Slobodan Milošević and the Republic of Yugoslavia in order to prevent the ethnic cleansing of Muslim and Albanian Kosovars.

Narrowing the cases to those that take place in the latter 20th century provides a more proximate evolving view of PLA thinking on contemporary warfare. Furthermore, events that have affected the PLA after the death of Mao Zedong in September 1976 are of particular importance due to the former leader's great hold and sway over Chinese military thought and development. After Mao's departure, it appears that senior PLA and CCP officials were better able to move away from dogmatic Maoist thought in general, and approaches to warfare in particular.

Additionally, as mentioned previously, the cases chosen here relate closely to more contemporary CCP concerns over its ability to defend and protect PRC sovereignty, especially in light of China's history with direct Western impositions against that sovereignty in the past. This makes the selection of cases such as the 1991 Gulf War and the 1999 Kosovo intervention appropriate given their similarity to core CCP sovereignty issues such as concerns over de facto Taiwanese independence, and international concerns over human rights issues tied to Muslim unrest in China's Xinjiang province.

To test these cases, the author chose five clear and measurable criteria that help describe a Western military approach to war fighting. The first is an emphasis on and reliance upon superior technology and force quality, as opposed to simply sheer mass and force size only. Manifestation of this characteristic is measured in the form of official pronouncements that are present, and associated actions that support such emphasis, such as the actual acquisition of more modern military means by the PLA.

The second characteristic is a focus on military discipline and modern training, as opposed to other non-military activities (e.g., political education). This is measured by testing for the presence of modern training events that have actually been conducted and their frequency during the relevant periods, as well as for institutional initiatives to increase the quality and education of PLA members to increase military professionalism and effectiveness.

The third characteristic of a Western way of war fighting that will be applied to the chosen cases is a demonstrated ability to change and adapt when presented with a changing security environment, as opposed to dogmatic adherence to military approaches and methods that no longer apply or lack utility. Much like the first characteristic, this is measured by testing for the presence and importance of official exhortations and pronouncements that stress the need to improve PLA modernization of its personnel and systems, and the presence of unofficial writings by current and former PLA officials and scholars that equally echo the need to modernize.

The fourth characteristic is the actual willingness to finance military development through fiscal allocation. This is measured by testing for any positive or negative change in defense spending. If present, a marked increase in fiscal spending that supports PLA modernization efforts will indicate the presence of this characteristic in the chosen cases. Any decrease, or little to no measured movement will fail to provide evidence regarding the presence of this characteristic.

The fifth and final characteristic is casualty aversion. Measuring this particular characteristic is difficult given the fact that the PLA has not been involved in actual combat since the 1979 Sino-Vietnamese conflict. However, much like with the first and third characteristics, the presence of official and unofficial exhortations, pronouncements, and doctrinal writings that stress the need to avoid incurring excessive casualties through the employment of modern systems will indicate the presence of this particular characteristic.

Table 1 lists these five criteria, along with the three historic cases mentioned. The intent of this and all subsequent tables throughout this monograph is to show how PLA attitudes and approaches toward warfare have trended toward becoming more Western since 1979.

Table 1. Western Characteristics of Warfare across Three Case Studies

WESTERN CHARACTERISTICS OF WARFARE	CASE STUDIES		
	1979-1990	1991-1998	2000-Today
	PLA Actions/Developments Post-Sino-Vietnamese Conflict	PLA Actions/Developments Post–U.S. Gulf War	PLA Actions/Developments Post-U.S./NATO Intervention in Kosovo
Emphasis Placed on Technology			
Emphasis on Discipline and Training			
Exhibited Willingness to Change/Learn/Adapt			
Allocation of Fiscal Resources in Support of Modernization			
Casualty Aversion			

Source: Created by author.

CASE STUDIES

By narrowing the selection of historic cases to those that occurred during the latter 20th century, this monograph seeks to provide a more proximate rationale behind PLA thinking on contemporary warfare. The first case considered examines PLA operations conducted against Vietnam in 1979, and how this particular event served to highlight PLA shortcomings, which spurred Westernization efforts. The second and third cases will examine PLA actions and initiatives that followed the U.S. military's Operation Desert Storm from 1990-1991, and NATO's Operation Allied Force against the Republic of Yugoslavia in 1999 to illustrate increased efforts by the PLA to Westernize in the wake of these modern conflicts.

The 1979 Sino-Vietnamese Conflict

The abysmal performance of the PLA during the 1979 Sino-Vietnamese conflict marked its nadir in modern times, and served as an impetus for increased military Westernization efforts. What resulted was a growing acceptance and realization by the PLA that it had to seek more Western approaches to war fighting to be effective in future conflicts.

By 1979, China believed that its "struggle against Soviet power in general and Vietnamese influence in particular was not going well," given Hanoi's increased influence in Cambodia, and Moscow's continued support for Hanoi.[46] The PRC perceived that the newly unified Socialist Republic of Vietnam was a threat to its ability to freely assert its sovereign interests in what Beijing considered its backyard. The result was Beijing's adoption of a strategy that sought to compel greater Vietnamese adherence to and respect for PRC regional influence, while forcing the eventual removal of the Socialist Republic of Vietnam from Cambodia, and to counter Soviet influence generally.

In order to achieve this strategic goal, PRC leaders decided that any military approach undertaken by the PLA would need to be short and decisive. With a limited and quick offensive operation against Vietnam, China hoped to "teach lessons to both Vietnam and the Soviet Union" by conducting "a razor-sharp" limited military action to "stem the tide of Soviet influence in East Asia" before the Soviet Union was able to increase support or mobilize against China.[47] Additionally, it would have to include lethal and rapid maneuver to quickly destroy targeted

---

[46]Segal, 212.

[47]Ibid., 216-217.

19

Vietnamese forces directly across the Sino-Vietnamese border before drawing in increased Soviet support.[48] After recently emerging from Mao's Cultural Revolution, the PLA, which was unfortunately more politically than professionally focused at this point, would now have to conduct military operations that it had neither the ability, nor the means to conduct.

Nevertheless, the PLA "had little room for error in a strategy highly dependent on the [relatively] surgical use of the military instrument."[49] However, "when the PLA [ultimately] failed to strike an impressive blow, [the overall] Chinese strategy collapsed."[50] The reasons for this failure are many, but all tied to poor performance.

By 1979, China's military power had decreased in quality and effectiveness compared to only a decade prior when it had been called into action against India in 1962.[51] By 1975, CMC officials, along with Deng Xiaoping believed the PLA "had become an aging, overstaffed, arrogant, obsolescent giant incapable of conducting modern warfare."[52]

One reason for this was that the PLA remained heavily reliant upon its aging Soviet equipment and creative efforts to keep it functioning.[53] By this time, China's defense industry

---

[48]Segal, 217.

[49]Ibid.

[50]Ibid.

[51]Ibid., 211.

[52]Paul H.B. Godwin, "Compensating for Deficiencies: Doctrinal Evolution in the Chinese People's Liberation Army 1978-1999," in *Seeking Truth from Facts : A Retrospective on Chinese Military Studies in the Post-Mao Era,* eds. James C. Mulvenon and Andrew N.D. Yang (Santa Monica, CA: National Security Research Division, RAND, 2001), 88.

[53]The Sino-Soviet split, which began in the early 1950s, continued well into the 1980s, and served to hamper PLA efforts to not only acquire more modern military technology, but to maintain the Soviet equipment it had on hand throughout this period. For details see Immanuel C.Y. Hsü, *The Rise of Modern China*, 6th ed. (New York, NY: Oxford University Press, 2000), 671-687; and Shambaugh, *Modernizing China's Military: Progress, Problems, and Prospects,* 226-228.

proved "capable only of building weapons and equipment based on Soviet technologies of the 1950s," and severely lacked the ability to research and develop the military means to fight and prevail in a more modern conflict against a more Westernized opponent.[54] This is because ". . . in the almost thirty years between the [Korean war, and the Sino-Vietnamese conflict,] little seemed to have improved in Chinese equipment and combat performance."[55] Furthermore, ". . . the specific tactics adopted by the PLA during the war were predetermined by . . . the well-known limitations of out-dated [sic] armed forces."[56]

As for the organization, command, and control of its forces during the Sino-Vietnamese conflict, the PLA established an ad hoc organizational structure by combining both the Kunming and Guangzhou military regional commands across China's southern border area. PLA commanders massed forces "from 10 [different] military regions, with the militia and frontier guards providing rear security and logistical support."[57] This equaled 20 divisions consisting of "300,000 soldiers, 7000-1000 aircraft, 1000 tanks, and 1500 pieces of heavy artillery," massed on the Sino-Vietnamese border, and all of which had never previously operated jointly.[58] Ultimately, the PLA ended up only attacking across the border with approximately 10 divisions in total, consisting of 80,000 soldiers, in a "largely set-piece" frontal assault along five axes against approximately 75,000-100,000 Vietnamese border and militia forces in well-established strongpoint defenses.[59]

---

[54]Mulvenon and Yang, 88.

[55]Segal, 218.

[56]Ibid.

[57]Ibid., 219.

[58]Ibid.

[59]Ibid.

PLA forces conducted human wave attacks in both mountainous and built-up areas that led to high casualties. Shortly after the attack was launched on 17 February, "the PLA quickly ground to a snail's pace."[60]

Having relied heavily upon its infantry forces, the PLA "by and large [fought] a one-dimensional war with [very little use of] tank [,air] and artillery support."[61] Additionally, "some of the most glaring problems in operations involved antiquated logistics and poor reconnaissance [with some reports stating that] Qing dynasty maps were used in some areas."[62] However, by keeping their military objectives somewhat limited to the border area around Lang Son, the PLA hoped to avoid putting itself in a position where its "logistics, equipment, and air defense[s]" would be severely wanting.[63] Seventeen days later, the PLA limped back across the border, claiming victory primarily due to a lack of perceived Soviet response to its actions.

In fact, it seems that the poor PLA performance, along with its limited objectives, prevented any perceived need by Moscow to increase its support to Hanoi. Instead, "China not only failed to teach the Soviet Union and the world a lesson about Soviet power," but also revealed its military shortcomings. The PRC "lost a great deal in the 1979 [Sino-Vietnamese] war, whether the balance sheet is measured in lives or political cost. But perhaps the greatest loss was in a more intangible product—China's reputation."[64]

---

[60]Segal, 219.

[61]Ibid., 220.

[62]Ibid.

[63]Ibid.

[64]Ibid., 227.

Most critically, the conflict also sparked the revelation within the PLA that it was currently unable to decisively secure PRC sovereign interests. Furthermore, the PLA acknowledged, "the war had 'lent a big impetus to the modernization of our army'."[65]

The Sino-Vietnamese conflict not only served as a great impetus for change, but it also served to move the PLA further away from a rigid and dogmatic adherence to Maoist people's war. Afterword, "Chinese defense policy planners [became] more pragmatic, ensuring [increased] modernization of PLA training and that at least certain services obtained [more modern] weapons."[66]

Another result that stemmed from this humiliating failure seems to have been a very real shift in PLA understanding of war fighting in a more modern era. In fact, this particular PLA experience is quite analogous to the conceptual shift that took place within the Prussian military after its defeat in 1806 against France at the Battle of Jena–Auerstädt.[67] As with the Prussian case, the Chinese military had to grapple with how best to change itself after experiencing defeat.

Nevertheless, after the Sino-Vietnamese conflict, the PLA realized its approach to war fighting had not worked, and that change was necessary in order to prepare for "a wide set of contingencies ranging from border conflicts to potentially high-intensity limited war."[68] This had the effect of pushing China's armed forces down a path away from the dogmatic application of Maoist people's war and toward becoming "a more flexible force capable of responding effectively to a wider range of contingencies than continental defense against [the Soviet

---

[65]*Liberation Army Daily,* quoted in Segal, 223.

[66]Ibid., 226.

[67]Peter Paret, *The Cognitive Challenge of War: Prussia 1806* (Princeton, NJ: Princeton University Press, 2009), 164.

[68]Mulvenon and Yang, 97.

Union].["69] As a result, many within the CCP and the PLA began to outwardly voice the position that people's war was no longer sufficient in providing the Chinese military with a suitable doctrine to counter more modern threats.

On 12 March 1980, Deng Xiaoping, at a CMC meeting, openly questioned "the excessively defensive posture of fighting adversaries deep inside China in a war of attrition."[70] Deng went on to clearly assert that attempting to lure potential enemies deep into China during a potential conflict in order to defeat them, as Mao's people's war advocated, was no longer relevant. Instead, he proposed what he called "people's war under modern conditions," which was to be a more "active" form of frontier defense.[71] Along with this change in terminology, came an increased emphasis by Deng and the CMC on "weaponry and technology instead of the human factor in war," which was a clear break from "a cardinal tenet of Maoist military thought."[72] There began to emerge within the PLA the view that Western characteristics, such as "modern technology, better connectivity, and improved command and control were necessary if the PLA were to prevail in modern war in the latter part of the twentieth century."[73]

This evolving view by the top leaders of China's military appears to have resonated. For example, Su Yu, a prominent and widely respected PLA official, stated at the time that the rigid application of Maoist military principles should be avoided, and instead suggested a more pragmatic approach "in the light of actual conditions."[74]

---

[69]Mulvenon and Yang, 97.

[70]Shambaugh, *Modernizing China's Military: Progress, Problems, and Prospects,* 62.

[71]Ibid.

[72]Ibid., 63.

[73]Wortzel, 22.

[74]Segal, 224.

However, while Deng Xiaoping and other like-minded Chinese leaders believed that military modernization was certainly necessary after the Sino-Vietnamese conflict, all agreed that for the time being, these efforts must be subordinated to the greater need to modernize China's agricultural, industrial, and science and technology sectors first. By this time, Deng had already begun "to replace Stalinist-style central planning with a market economy and to open the country to foreign trade and investment," the PRC could not afford to "spend much on fancy military equipment."[75] Instead, Deng's intent was to increase spending on PLA modernization as the PRC economy grew overtime.

In a speech given to the CMC in June 1985, Deng stated:

> The four modernizations include the modernization of defense. Without that modernization there would be only three [agriculture, industry, and science and technology]. But the four modernizations should be achieved in order of priority. Only when we have a good economic foundation will it be possible for us to modernize the army's equipment.[76]

The result was that "after 1979 there were more clear cut emphasis within the PLA on those aspects of modernization that did not cost a great deal of money, for example in training and professional skills."[77]

Both Xu Xiangqian, China's defense minister at the time, and Xiao Ke, who had been given the responsibility to revitalize PLA "research centers and professional military education," viewed the PLA as unable to "meet the demands of modern war."[78] Both sought to revamp institutions such as the PLA Academy of Military Science in an effort to "[emancipate] the minds

---

[75]Susan L. Shirk, *China: Fragile Superpower* (Oxford, NY: Oxford University Press, 2007), 15, 21.

[76]Xiaoping Deng, "Speech at an Enlarged Meeting of the Military Commission of the Central Committee of the Communist Party of China," People's Daily Online, 4 June 1985, http://english.peopledaily.com.cn/dengxp/vol3/text/c1410.html (accessed 5 February 2014).

[77]Segal, 225.

[78]Mulvenon and Yang, 90-91.

of PLA strategist—freeing them from stultifying consequences of literal dependence on Mao Zedong's writings."[79] Additionally, both Xu and Xiao advocated for greater development of combined and joint operations, both within the ground forces of the PLA, and across the branches. Later, "observations by Chinese military strategists of other conflicts, particularly the British defeat of Argentine forces in the Falkland Islands in 1982, contributed to the perceived need to modernize military doctrine in China," especially given the similarity of this conflict with a potential one that could occur over a de facto deceleration of independence by Taipei with support from Washington.[80] Official CCP analyses and pronouncements like these, along with the creation of institutions like the Academy of Military Science in order to increase the training quality of the PLA, provide further evidence of increasing Westernization, along with an apparent willingness to change from within the highest ranks of China's military establishment.

As the PLA moved into the 1980s, it began to develop a military strategy that framed local, limited war as a specific type of conflict to "assert one's own standpoint and will through limited military action."[81] Within this strategy, a more modern PLA operating doctrine soon developed that emphasized "rapid response by forces maintained at a high level of readiness," along with "increased emphasis on mobility, lethality, intelligence, and command and control coordinating swiftly, moving joint service operations to quickly terminate war."[82]

By 1985, the PLA was preparing itself to fight and win local and limited wars primarily on China's vast periphery. As a result, the PLA moved further away from a purely defensive people's war approach it had clung onto, and began to "experiment with mobile, integrated

---

[79]Mulvenon and Yang, 90.

[80]Wortzel, 22.

[81]Jiao Wu and Xiao Hui, "Modern Limited War Calls for Reform of Traditional Military Principles," *Guofang Daxue Xuebao* (November 1987), quoted in Mulvenon and Yang, 98.

[82]Ibid., 97.

warfare" along Western lines.[83] Fighting and winning against a technologically superior Western military foe like the U.S., in a dispute over Taiwan for example, would require an offensive capability that incorporated more modern and Western operating concepts, along with the modern means to carry them out.

Later in the decade, the PLA began to conduct training exercises in order to improve its interoperability between its different branches. These exercises focused on specific regions and "involved air, ground, naval, and special operations units," but suffered from a "lack of coordination" between the participating units.[84] Additionally, the PLA struggled throughout much of the decade to develop integrated logistical systems that could support units in the field, instead of having them default back to "the old Maoist emphasis on unit-based 'self-reliance'."[85] However, the fact that the PLA did change its approaches to training in order to develop more modern military competencies, supports the assertion of increasing Westernization.

Additionally, the PLA now actively sought to acquire and domestically develop modern military hardware and systems. However, a lack of technological and scientific capacity severely limited PLA advances. While attempting to "selectively purchase key systems" from some European suppliers, it appears the PLA's self-reliant approach to development yielded little success largely because of its collective inability to replicate and reproduce those prototype systems it was able to acquire.[86] However, as with training, efforts like these do support the idea of an increasingly Westernized PLA, albeit in its nascent stages.

---

[83]Wortzel, 22.

[84]Shambaugh, *Modernizing China's Military: Progress, Problems, and Prospects*, 98.

[85]Ibid., 99.

[86]Ibid., 230.

Nevertheless, there is no evidence to suggest that the PRC significantly increased its fiscal allocation toward military modernization in the wake of the Sino-Vietnamese conflict. Growth of China's gross domestic product (GDP) throughout the 1980s averaged nine percent, and the PRC spent just two percent of its GDP annually on defense.[87] This relatively low allocation is because the Chinese economy had just begun to open up to the larger global market, along with the collective perception held by many within the CCP and PLA of an overall improved security situation. While war with the Soviet Union or the U.S. was certainly possible, many of China's top leaders now believed it was unlikely, Deng included. The result was that for now, much of the PRC budgetary allocation went toward modernizing China's agricultural, industrial, and science and technological capacities.[88]

Given this fiscal reality, the emphasis by the PLA by the mid-1980s shifted to "economizing in the armed forces" in order to increase available funds.[89] One result of this was the reduction of approximately one million enlisted personnel in 1985 in order to streamline the massive number of soldiers in the ground forces, and free funding for the acquisition of modern military hardware.[90] The PLA also reduced the number of its military regions from 11 to seven, while also trimming "the numbers of units in general departments, services, and branches."[91]

---

[87]Shambaugh, *Modernizing China's Military: Progress, Problems, and Prospects,* 191; and The World Bank, "Data: GDP Growth (Annual %)," The World Bank Group, http://data.worldbank.org/country/china (accessed 9 March 2014).

[88]Joffe, 48-62.

[89]Ibid.

[90]Timothy Heath, "Restructuring the Military: Drivers and Prospects for Xi's Top-Down Reforms," The Jamestown Foundation, http://www.jamestown.org/programs/chinabrief/single/?tx_ttnews%5Btt_news%5D=41936&tx_ttnews%5BbackPid%5D=25&cHash=12cb9c60b4b918bb7d80cfef503069d1#.UwpwuHm3T4g (accessed 22 February 2014).

[91]Ibid.

Additionally, the CMC authorized the PLA to "go into business . . . to offset and compensate for low levels of state allocations."[92] However, while these commercial activities helped somewhat in financing PLA activities, they also had the "very deleterious effect of soldiers spending time in unprofessional business activity (much of it illegal) instead of training."[93]

In summary, the abysmal performance of the PLA during the 1979 Sino-Vietnamese conflict marked the nadir for the Maoist operating concept of people's war, and served as a point of departure toward greater Westernization of the PLA. As seen in table 2, three out of the five characteristics of a Western way of warfare clearly manifest themselves in this case.

Table 2. Manifestation of Western Characteristics of
Warfare Post-Sino-Vietnamese Conflict

WESTERN CHARACTERISTICS OF WARFARE	CASE STUDIES
	1979 - 1990
	PLA Actions/Developments Post-Sino-Vietnamese Conflict
Emphasis Placed on Technology	Yes
Emphasis on Discipline and Training	Yes
Exhibited Willingness to Change/Learn	Yes
Allocation of Economic Resources in Support of Modernization	No
Casualty Aversion	No

Source: Created by author.

Specifically, the PLA realized that, in light of its performance against the Vietnamese military, it would likely fail to defend China's other core sovereign interests against a relatively

---

[92]Shambaugh, *Modernizing China's Military: Progress, Problems, and Prospects,* 184.

[93]Ibid.

more modernized military threat, such as the U.S. in a dispute over Taiwan. As a result, official CCP and PLA pronouncements and actions in the wake of the Sino-Vietnamese conflict increasingly called for and directed the gradual acquisition of more modern military equipment and methods in order to counter military weakness. A purely defensive Maoist people's war approach was out, and a more active defense, in the form of "people's war under modern conditions" was in.[94]

As a result, the PLA had no choice but to seek more low-cost (i.e., training and professional education) modernization efforts due to other fiscal priorities. This involved an increased emphasis by PLA officials on training and personnel improvement in order to meet the demands of a more modern form of war fighting. For now, the PLA would primarily invest more in its human capital, organization, and tactics, while acquiring what it could in terms of hardware.

Additionally, there appears to have been no discussion within the PLA of avoiding casualties in the wake of the Sino-Vietnamese conflict. However, much of the evidence discussed here does support the manifestation of a sincere willingness on the part of the PLA to change, adapt, and learn from this particular failure, all of which helped spur further movement by the PLA toward a more Western-like approach to war fighting.

The 1990-1991 Gulf War

The 1990-1991 U.S. led conflict against Saddam Hussein's Iraq significantly shaped PLA thinking. It also served as one of the primary and most proximate impetuses behind PLA movement toward greater Westernization.

After 1989, the PLA was excluded from Western military technologies and exchanges because of sanctions that had been imposed on the PRC by the U.S. and other European countries

---

[94]Shambaugh, *Modernizing China's Military: Progress, Problems, and Prospects,* 62-66.

30

after the CCP crackdown against demonstrators in June 1989 in Tiananmen Square in Beijing.[95]

Within this context, and feeling somewhat isolated diplomatically and militarily vulnerable, the

U.S.-led coalition response to Iraq's 1990 invasion of Kuwait sent PLA officials reeling. Because

of this conflict, the PLA's movement away from a dogmatic following of Maoist military

thought, and toward a more Western one would continue, albeit with more vigor.

On 2 August 1990, the Iraqi military, consisting largely of Soviet equipped forces,

invaded Kuwait, provoking the ire of many nations, especially the U.S. The actions of Saddam's

Iraq were "a clear threat to the great oilfields of eastern Arabia and virtually forced the West—led

by the United States—to react."[96] Because of its diplomatic and military power, Washington,

much to the consternation of Beijing, was able to assemble a military coalition with United

Nations support. However, it was the rapidity and overwhelming effectiveness of the U.S.

response that most concerned the PLA.

Within 34 hours of U.S. President George Bush's order, "forty-eight F-15C air

superiority fighters" arrived in Saudi Arabia, and a brigade from the 82nd Airborne Division was

on the ground by 9 August.[97] By January 1991, the U.S. military had moved approximately

500,000 personnel and 3,700,000 tons of cargo, "roughly the equivalent of the population of

Denver, Colorado . . . a third of the way around the world."[98] U.S. and coalition mechanized and

airmobile forces, along with "devastating levels of air power . . . [attacked] . . . deep into the flank

---

[95]Shambaugh, *Modernizing China's Military: Progress, Problems, and Prospects,* 21; and Dennis J Blasko, *Chinese Army Today: Tradition and Transformation for the 21st Century* (New York, NY: Routledge, 2006),164.

[96]Robert Michael Citino, *Blitzkrieg to Desert Storm: The Evolution of Operational Warfare* (Lawrence, KS: University Press of Kansas, 2004), 276.

[97]Ibid., 277.

[98]Ibid., 278.

of the Iraqi positions, catching the defenders unprepared."[99] In the end, "the U.S.-led coalition

fought the battle of maneuver nearly to perfection," and Saddam Hussein's war-making

capabilities were "shattered," with very little cost to the U.S.-led coalition.[100]

The outcome utterly shocked the PLA. Prior to the conflict, "PLA analysis had predicted

that U.S. forces would become bogged down in a ground war" based upon "the PLA's study of

the Soviet experience in Afghanistan and on the Iran-Iraq conflict."[101] PLA officials were

particularly disturbed "when they saw the way that the United States and its allies used high-

technology weapons, mobility, and join operations to collapse and defeat Iraq's armed forces."[102]

David Shambaugh provides a comprehensive listing of PLA concerns:

> Nearly every aspect of the campaign reminded the PLA High Command of its
> deficiencies: electronic warfare; precision-guided munitions; stealth technology;
> precision bombing of military targets with minimized collateral damage; the sheer
> numbers of sorties flown, with minimal lass of attack aircraft and life; campaign
> coordination through airborne command and control systems; the deployment of attack
> aircraft from half a world away using in-flight refueling; the use of satellites in targeting
> and intelligence gathering; space-based early warning and surveillance; the use of
> command centers in the United states to coordinate Patriot anti-missile defenses in Saudi
> Arabia and Israel; the massive naval flotilla assembled in the Gulf; the airlift and rapid
> deployment capability; the maintenance of high-tempo operations; the ability of troops to
> exist in desert conditions; modern logistics; information warfare and the ability to 'blind'
> Iraqi intelligence and defenses; and so on.[103]

After the conflict ended, Jiang Zemin, then head of the CMC and later PRC president,

initiated a number of conferences and studies in order to thoroughly study and learn from the

---

[99]Citino, 287.

[100]Ibid., 287-288.

[101]Shambaugh, *Modernizing China's Military: Progress, Problems, and Prospects*, 69.

[102]Wortzel, 23.

[103]Shambaugh, *Modernizing China's Military: Progress, Problems, and Prospects*, 69-70.

U.S.-led military action against Iraq.[104] What Jiang and others soon realized was that the PLA had to become more modern in its means and approaches to waging a modern form of warfare as exhibited by the U.S. While this effort to modernize began in the 1980s, many Chinese officials believed that it would now have to gain greater momentum.

PLA symposia resulted in a wide range of PLA pronouncements and publications that keenly analyzed the 1990-1991 Gulf War, and supported increased modernization efforts. Within such forums, many prominent PLA theorists, such as Xiong Guangkai, viewed the U.S. military performance as a true revolution in military affairs.[105] Xiong placed emphasis on what he considered to be "new trends" in waging modern warfare such as improving the quality of a military instead of relying on sheer quantity; leveraging "smart weaponry," and "information technology-based equipment" in order to offset quantity further; ensuring that air and naval forces, and not only land forces, receive adequate funding; and placing a higher priority on the "development of hi-tech branches," such as "military space force[s], missile units and missile defense units, electronic warfare units and information warfare units."[106]

As China's president, Jiang Zemin emphasized the need to improve the overall quality, in men and material, of the PLA, while reducing its size. By 1997, the PLA had cut approximately 500,000 personnel from its ranks.[107] Additionally, the PLA created the General Armaments

---

[104]Guangkai Xiong, *Guo Ji Zhan LüE Yu Xin Jun Shi Bian Ge - International Strategy and Revolution in Military Affairs*, Di 1 ban. ed. (Beijing, China: Qing hua da xue chu ban she, 2003), 179.

[105]Xiong, 168-172; Michael Pillsbury, *Chinese Views of Future Warfare*, ed. Michael Pillsbury (Washington, DC: National Defense University Press, 1998), 249-420; and Kamphausen et al., 12-13.

[106]Xiong, 171-172.

[107]Heath.

Department to oversee weapons and equipment develop and research, and link China's civilian factories with its defense industry.[108]

Major General Wang Zhenxi echoed the importance of modernizing the PLA, especially precision weaponry, and electronic warfare capabilities, along with the need for survival systems that included an integrated command control network system that could withstand a modern assault.[109] General Wang was the director of the Foreign Military Studies Division at the PLA Academy of Military Science at the time of the Gulf War, and was responsible for briefing a number of high-level PLA officials on the conflict and the PLA's views of it.

Furthermore, General Fu Quanyou, then commander of the Lanzhou military region and later director of the PLA General Logistics Department, recognized that the PLA must learn to fight jointly, by integrating all of its services, as the American military had done. In his view, a Western way of waging war was "five-dimensional," and involved "land, sea and air forces, as well as space and electronic technologies."[110]

In short, the U.S. led conflict against Iraq, and its subsequent study and analysis by the PLA brought about "a thorough revision of operational doctrine and training in the PLA" that was to result in a "new doctrine of 'limited war under high-technology conditions'."[111] This "broad theoretical examination of the revolution of military affairs inside PLA academic centers," and among the top members of China's military soon resulted in "a military-wide effort to modernize the force and field the capabilities the PLA was seen to lack."[112] Therefore, it is clear that many of

---

[108]Blasko, *Chinese Army Today: Tradition and Transformation for the 21st Century* (2012), 30.

[109]Shambaugh, *Modernizing China's Military: Progress, Problems, and Prospects,* 72.

[110]Ibid., 73.

[111]Ibid., 70.

[112]Wortzel, 23.

the characteristics emphasized within these official pronouncements and efforts are quite consistent with those that constitute a Western way of waging warfare.

After the Gulf War, China's defense industry began to focus its research and development efforts into acquiring advanced weaponry. Priority was on:

> Mastering electronic warfare and electronic countermeasures (particularly air and naval countermeasures); improving ballistic missile production and precision-guided munitions (PGMs); building satellites, early warning and command systems, and advanced communication relay stations; investigating laser technologies; developing artificial intelligence and information warfare skills, improving avionics and mastering in-flight refueling; and developing anti-ballistic missile systems.[113]

The PLA also began to increase the frequency of training exercises that placed a greater emphasis on combined and joint operations between the different parts of the army, and between the army and the other branches of the PLA. Exercises conducted between 1993 and 1995 in particular, "involved some combination of different ground force units (armor, infantry, anti-chemical, heliborne, etc.), as well as multiservice joint exercises."[114] In addition, in 1994, PLA units from the Nanjing military region, directly across the Taiwan Strait, conducted amphibious landings with naval support from the People's Liberation Army Navy. The pace of these particular exercises increased in scale between 1995 and 1996, and involved "live firing from ships, tanks, and bombers" along with ballistic missile supporting attacks by the PLA Second Artillery.[115]

Finally, it appears that there was also a marked increase in spending on defense, beginning in 1994. China's GDP grew from approximately $379 billion to $1 trillion between 1991 and 1999, a total growth of approximately 163 percent.[116] However, China's defense budget

---

[113]Shambaugh, *Modernizing China's Military: Progress, Problems, and Prospects,* 70.

[114]Ibid., 99.

[115]Ibid., 100.

[116]The World Bank.

grew from approximately $11.3 billion in 1991 to $39.5 billion in 1999—a 250 percent

increase.[117] Clearly, China increased its defense spending significantly because of overall

economic growth.

These increases greatly assisted PLA efforts to, among other things, acquire and

incorporate advance weapon systems across the land, naval, and air braches. Increased spending

also led to improvements in mechanized vehicles, air defenses, aviation platforms, and the PLA's

nuclear arsenal. However, the PLA also began to develop and test "a more robust space-based

communications and intelligence architecture [that included] integrated satellites and precision

guidance" of its weapon systems, along with other similar-improvements that sought to increase

the capabilities of "joint operations across the domains of warfare." [118]

To summarize, the PLA was both surprised and disturbed by the relatively rapid and

overwhelming effective military response by the U.S. As a result, the 1990-1991 U.S. led conflict

against Saddam Hussein's Iraq significantly shaped PLA thinking, and served as one of the

primary and most proximate impetuses behind PLA movement toward greater Westernization.

In the wake of the conflict, China's political and military leaders thoroughly studied and

analyzed the conflict in order to learn how the PLA could improve the overall quality of its war

fighting capabilities. These efforts included conferences and published papers that strongly

advocated for a need to modernize the PLA along Western lines.

Additionally, the PRC increased budgetary allocation in support of increased PLA

modernization efforts that included the development and acquisition of advanced weaponry and

---

[117]Institute for Strategic Studies, *The Military Balance* (London, England: Institute for Strategic Studies, 1991), 244; Institute for Strategic Studies, *The Military Balance* (London, England: Institute for Strategic Studies, 1992), 258; Institute for Strategic Studies, *The Military Balance* (London, England: Institute for Strategic Studies, 1995), 320; and Institute for Strategic Studies, *The Military Balance* (London, England: Institute for Strategic Studies, 2001), 322.

[118]Wortzel, 23.

systems. Furthermore, the PLA sought to improve its professional training and discipline by placing a greater emphasis on combined and joint operations both between the different parts of the land forces, and between the land forces and the other branches of the PLA. Finally, much like the previous case, it appears there was no discussion of casualty avoidance within the PLA through this period.

As Table 3 below indicates, the PLA exhibited four out of the five characteristics associated with a Western style of warfare. Therefore, PLA attitudes and approaches toward warfare have continued to trend toward becoming more Western in the wake of the U.S. led 1990-1991 Gulf War against Iraq.

Table 3. Manifestation of Western Characteristics of Warfare
Post-U.S.-led 1990-1991 Gulf War against Iraq

WESTERN CHARACTERISTICS OF WARFARE	CASE STUDIES
	1991-1998
	PLA Actions/Developments Post–U.S. Gulf War
Emphasis Placed on Technology	Yes
Emphasis on Discipline and Training	Yes
Exhibited Willingness to Change/Learn	Yes
Allocation of Economic Resources in Support of Modernization	Yes
Casualty Aversion	No

Source: Created by author.

U.S. and NATO Military Action against the Republic of Yugoslavia

Much like the previous case, U.S. and NATO military action against the Republic of Yugoslavia also served as a strong motivating force that has further reinforced PLA efforts to become increasingly Western-like in its approach to war fighting. A central reason is that this case, like the 1990-1991 Gulf War before it, provoked similar concerns over the PRC's perceived inability to defend and protect core Chinese sovereign interests.

37

From March through June 1999, a the U.S. and NATO member countries conducted a predominantly air-centric military campaign named Operation Allied Force (hereafter Allied Force) against President Slobodan Milosevic and the FRY in order to counter Serbian efforts to ethnically cleanse and remove Muslim Kosovars from Kosovo. It is this particular justification for military intervention (i.e., concerns over human rights violations) on the part of the U.S. and NATO members that is both central to CCP and PLA concerns in this particular case, and continued to spur further adoption by the PLA of those characteristics that contribute to a Western approach to war fighting.

Much like today, the PRC government during this period had been widely criticized by the U.S., along with other Western governments and groups for its treatment of the non-Han Uighur Muslim population in Xinjiang province.[119] With some in this Uighur Muslim population calling for a separate and autonomous region, Beijing had long sought to increase its control over the region in order to counter such calls for independence. Matters like these, remain central, or "core" issues that tie directly to Chinese perceptions about its sovereignty.[120]

Within this context, many Chinese political and military officials were highly concerned about the potential for Western governments to draw a similarity between the situations in Xinjiang and Kosovo. In the minds of China's political and military leadership, human rights concerns held by the West relating to restive Muslim minority populations in China, much like in

---

[119]Human Rights Watch, "China: Human Rights Concerns in Xinjiang," Human Rights Watch, October 2001, http://www.hrw.org/reports/2001/10/18/china-human-rights-concerns-xinjiang (accessed 22 February 2014); and Dewardric L. McNeal, Congressional Research Service Report for Congress, *China's Relations with Central Asian States and Problems of Terrorism,* Policy Archives, 17 December 2001, http://research.policy.archive.org/1315.pdf (accessed 22 February 2014).

[120]Michael D. Swaine, "China's Assertive Behavior-Part One: On 'Core Interests'," *China Leadership Monitor,* no. 34 (2011): 1-25, http://www.hoover.org/publications/china-leadership-monitor (accessed 22 February 2014).

the Kosovo case, could lead to a similar U.S.-led case for military intervention against the Chinese government.

When comparing the 1990-1991 Gulf War with Allied Force, it seems that many PLA analyses viewed the former as having "some characteristics of modern high-tech war, [while] the latter was [viewed as] a truly modern high-tech war with 'hyperconventional'[sic] features that must be analyzed and digested if the PRC were to be able to defend itself properly."[121] Furthermore, it appears that the PLA viewed Allied Force more "as a validation of [its] earlier assessments of the trends in modern warfare," which served to add momentum to Westernization efforts in order to counter a potentially similar U.S.-led military operation. [122]

Many of the trends in PLA modernization and training that discussed in the wake of the 1991 Gulf War appear to have continued after Allied Force. For example, the PLA further reduced overall force size by another 200,000, particularly in the land forces, while continuing its focus on improving the training and overall quality of its personnel.[123] Additionally, the PLA introduced "joint operations command institutions and systems" into its command structure within its military regions.[124]

---

[121]June Teufel Dreyer, *The PLA and the Kosovo Conflict* (Carlisle Barracks, PA: Strategic Studies Institute, U.S. Army War College, 2000), 4-5.

[122]U.S. Department of Defense (DOD), *Report to Congress Pursuant to the FY2000 National Defense Authorization Act, Annual Report on the Military Power of the People's Republic of China*, U.S. Department of Defense, 2002, http://www.defense.gov/news/Jul2002/d20020712china.pdf (accessed 22 February 2014), 12.

[123]The PLA increased is educational standards in certain key branches of the PLA, such as the Second Artillery, which has primary responsibility for China's nuclear and conventional missile forces. Additionally, the PLA conducted a number of personnel reduction efforts that continued throughout the 2000s. For specifics, see Jacqueline Newmyer, "The Revolution in Military Affairs with Chinese Characteristics," *Journal of Strategic Studies* 33, no. 4 (2010): 499; U.S. Department of Defense (DOD), *Annual Report to Congress: Military Power of the People's Republic of China 2006,* U.S. Department of Defense, 2006, http://www.defense.gov/pubs/pdfs/China%20Report%202006.pdf (accessed 22 February 2014), 5; and Heath.

[124]Heath.

Training efforts began to include "increased interaction and cooperation with foreign militaries" in order to assist in modernization efforts.[125] Additionally, U.S. and NATO success against the FRY has served to confirm the PLA's decision "to improve its joint operations capability by developing advanced [command, control, intelligence, surveillance, and reconnaissance] systems and improving inter-service cooperation."[126] Lastly, the PLA continued to develop aerial refueling, airborne early warning and collection, and electronic countermeasure aircraft, along with increasing its surface and subsurface naval forces in order to improve its ability to "secure vital sea lines of communication and/or key geostrategic terrain."[127]

The PLA also noticed that Serbian forces "suffered from inferior equipment, inadequate defense of civilian installations, and poor logistics."[128] Additionally, the PLA began development of its "Three Attacks, Three Defenses" air defense plan, which concentrated on successfully "attacking stealth aircraft, cruise missiles, and helicopters, while defending against precision strikes, electronic warfare, and enemy reconnaissance."[129] As a result, the PLA responded by placing even greater emphasis on developing its underground facilities, landline communications,

---

[125]U.S. Department of Defense (DOD), *FY04 Report to Congress on PRC Military Power Pursuant to the FY2000 National Defense Authorization Act, Annual Report on the Military Power of the People's Republic of China,* U.S. Department of Defense, 2004, http://www. defense.gov/pubs/d20040528PRC.pdf (accessed 22 February 2014), 5.

[126]U.S. Department of Defense (DOD), *FY04 Report to Congress on PRC Military Power Pursuant to the FY2000 National Defense Authorization Act, Annual Report on the Military Power of the People's Republic of China,* 4.

[127]Ibid., 5; and U.S. DOD, *Annual Report to Congress: Military Power of the People's Republic of China 2006,* 1.

[128]U.S. DOD, *Report to Congress Pursuant to the FY2000 National Defense Authorization Act, Annual Report on the Military Power of the People's Republic of China,* 2002, 12.

[129]Ibid., 12-13.

and well-concealed supply depots."[130] This also drove PLA efforts to both acquire and develop

technologically capable military systems that could perform such tasks, and incorporate them into

combined and joint training exercises.

The PLA keenly noticed the ability of the U.S. Air Force to send strategic bombing assets

half way around the world from bases within the continental U.S. to attack Serbian forces with

global positioning system guided precision munitions, such as the Joint Direct Attack

Munition.[131] Additionally, the U.S. Navy displayed its sea based strike capability when it

delivered sea and air launched cruise missiles with precision, and well outside the range of

Serbian forces.[132] Perhaps a more important observation by the PLA in the aftermath of Allied

Force was the apparent need for a vastly more effective operational and strategic offensive

capability to counter a similar attack by either the U.S. or a similarly more modernized opponent

like Japan's Self Defense Forces or the Republic of China (ROC) military. The result was an

increased effort by the PLA to increase its modernization efforts on developing the capability to

conduct "offensive operations against targets at the operational and strategic level of warfare"

that include "offensive strike assets," much like the U.S. military had demonstrated in Kosovo.[133]

---

[130]U.S. DOD, *Report to Congress Pursuant to the FY2000 National Defense Authorization Act, Annual Report on the Military Power of the People's Republic of China*, 2002, 12.

[131]Secretary of Defense and Chairman of the Joint Chiefs of Staff, Report to Congress, *Operation Allied Force: After-Action Report*, U.S. Department of Defense, 31 January 2000, http://www.dod.mil/pubs/kaar02072000.pdf (accessed 22 February 2014), xxiii, 79.

[132]Ibid., 91-92, 93.

[133]U.S. DOD, *Report to Congress Pursuant to the FY2000 National Defense Authorization Act, Annual Report on the Military Power of the People's Republic of China*, 2002, 13.

Some within the PLA referred to this more modern form of warfare as "non-contact warfare," and emphasized the need for improved PLA "precision, invisibility, and knowledge."[134] Faculty members at China's National Defense University called for the PLA to "develop innovative military theories, disengage ourselves from the traditional contact war mode, and break new ground in joint operation, in integrated air and outer space warfare, and in information network warfare."[135]

Soon after the U.S. and NATO military operation against the FRY, the PLA began to emphasize "operations that [would] paralyze the high-tech enemy's ability to conduct its campaign."[136] Beginning in the spring of 2000, senior PLA officials advocated for a coercive air campaign strategy, much like the one that occurred in Kosovo, that would include targeting not only military targets with high tech missiles and aircraft, but also critical infrastructure, oil depots, power plants, and transportation networks.[137] Additionally, in January 2007, the PLA successfully tested a direct ascent, anti-satellite weapon system that was able to destroy an aging weather satellite in low-Earth orbit.[138] Furthermore, the PLA development of an anti-ship ballistic missile displays further modernization efforts in order to develop an operational "non-contact"

---

[134]Newmyer, 495.

[135]Ibid., 495-496.

[136]U.S. DOD, *Report to Congress Pursuant to the FY2000 National Defense Authorization Act, Annual Report on the Military Power of the People's Republic of China*, 2002, 13.

[137]Mulvenon and Finkelstein, 234.

[138]U.S. Department of Defense, *Annual Report to Congress: Military Power of the People's Republic of China 2008,* U.S. Department of Defense, 2008, http://www.defense.gov/pubs/pdfs/China_Military_Report_08.pdf (accessed 22 February 2014), 3.

capability to "attack large ships, including aircraft carriers, in the western Pacific Ocean."[139] It becomes quite clear that military developments like these, along with ongoing improvements in China's nuclear strike capabilities, were spurred on by Allied Force, and afford the PRC with "a way to signal the ability to disrupt American civilian and military operations."[140]

Rather than focusing solely on the defense, the PLA now sought the ability to become a military force that could effectively strike at an enemy's will to resist with precision, and from afar.[141] In 2000, then-Senior Colonel Chen Bojian, emphasized that maintaining an effective offensive capability "has an extraordinary importance on the high-tech battlefield."[142] Chen also states:

> No enemy would 'let themselves so easily be involved in a protracted war with China,' though China might be defeated, because of the excessive cost of campaigning. Moreover, given overall Chinese strategy, 'it is also unallowable to have a protracted war. Under the conditions of a new history [(i.e., after Operation ALLIED FORCE)], the main task of the country is to carry out the economic construction . . . military actions must be quickly accomplished in scope and time.[143]

This is a crucial point that further supports how the PLA has incrementally departed from the purely defensive and protracted approach of Maoist people's war toward a more Westernized PLA approach that emphasizes technology, quality, and high tempo modern war fighting.

---

[139]U.S. Department of Defense (DOD), *Annual Report to Congress: Military and Security Developments Involving the People's Republic of China 2011,* U.S. Department of Defense, 2011, http://www.defense.gov/pubs/pdfs/2011_cmpr_final.pdf (accessed 22 February 2014), 3.

[140]Newmyer, 500; and U.S. DOD, *Annual Report to Congress: Military Power of the People's Republic of China 2006,* 3-4.

[141]U.S. DOD, *Report to Congress Pursuant to the FY2000 National Defense Authorization Act, Annual Report on the Military Power of the People's Republic of China,* 2002, 13.

[142]Charles F. Hawkins, "The People's Liberation Army Looks to the Future," *JFQ: Joint Force Quarterly,* no. 25 (2000): 16.

[143]Ibid.

Lastly, the trend of increased defense spending that began in the wake of the Gulf War and throughout the 1990s continued unabated after Allied Force. From 2001 to 2010, the PRC's GDP grew 353 percent from approximately $1.3 trillion to $5.9 trillion.[144] Additionally, during the same period the PLA's budget appears to have increased approximately 150 percent.[145] In 2002, the PRC announced publicly that its total-related military spending was $20 billion, with actual U.S. Department of Defense estimates placing it closer to $65 billion.[146] In 2006, the PRC announced that it would increase its defense allocation "by 14.7 percent, to approximately $35 billion."[147] U.S. intelligence agencies estimated the actual figure to be "between $70 billion and $105 billion . . . two to three times the announced budget."[148] Just two years later, the U.S. Department of Defense estimated that China's total-related military spending was "between $105 billion and $150 billion."[149] That said, the latest estimates by the U.S. government state that the PRC defense budget grew at an average rate of 9.7 percent per year between 2003 through 2013,

---

[144]The World Bank.

[145]U.S. DOD, *Annual Report to Congress: Military and Security Developments Involving the People's Republic of China 2011*, 41; and U.S. Department of Defense (DOD), *Annual Report to Congress: Military and Security Developments Involving the People's Republic of China 2010*, U.S. Department of Defense, 2010, http://www.defense.gov/pubs/pdfs/2010_cmpr_final.pdf (accessed 22 February 2014), 41-43.

[146]U.S. DOD, *Report to Congress Pursuant to the FY2000 National Defense Authorization Act, Annual Report on the Military Power of the People's Republic of China*, 2002, 2.

[147]U.S. DOD, *Annual Report to Congress: Military Power of the People's Republic of China 2006,* 19-20.

[148]Ibid.

[149]U.S. Department of Defense, *Annual Report to Congress: Military Power of the People's Republic of China 2009,* U.S. Department of Defense, 2009, http://www.defense.gov/pubs/pdfs/china_military_power_report_2009.pdf (accessed 22 February 2014), 31-32.

and that the current estimated amount for military-related expenditures is currently "between $135 billion and $215 billion."[150]

Regardless of the exact amount, it is clear that the PLA has benefitted significantly from China's rapid GDP growth through the 2000s. Additionally, it appears that the majority of the PLA budget during this period, somewhere between two to four percent of GDP went to further modernizing its land, naval, and air forces, along with developing its space and cyber systems.[151] The result of these budget increases has made the PLA the highest funded military force when compared to the militaries of other regional powers.[152]

In summary, there is clear evidence to support the assertion that the U.S. and NATO military action against the FRY significantly shaped PLA thinking, and served as one of the primary and most proximate impetuses behind continued PLA movement toward greater Westernization. Because of the perceived similarities between this case and to the restive Muslim minority populations in China, PRC and PLA officials feared that a future case for war could be made against the Chinese government. Therefore, the PLA viewed Operation Allied Force with an intense interest that confirmed much of its earlier assessments and validated its modernization efforts along Western lines in order to counter a potentially similar U.S.-led military operation.

---

[150]U.S. DOD, *Annual Report to Congress: Military and Security Developments Involving the People's Republic of China 2013,* 45-46.

[151]Ibid.; U.S. DOD, *Annual Report to Congress: Military and Security Developments Involving the People's Republic of China 2010,* 41-43; U.S. Department of Defense, *Annual Report to Congress: Military Power of the People's Republic of China 2007*, U.S. Department of Defense, 2007, http://www.defense.gov/pubs/pdfs/070523-China-Military-Power-final.pdf (accessed 22 February 2014), 25-26; Blasko, *Chinese Army Today: Tradition and Transformation for the 21st Century* (2006), 121-143; and Dennis J Blasko, *Chinese Army Today: Tradition and Transformation for the 21st Century* (2012), 148-174.

[152]For a comparison of state defense budgets within the region, see U.S. DOD, *Annual Report to Congress: Military and Security Developments Involving the People's Republic of China 2013,* 46.

While the PLA continued to focus on modernizing its systems and improving its force quality and structure, it also realized that it required a vastly more effective and Westernized operational and strategic offensive capability to counter a potential attack similar to those conducted by the U.S. military in Kosovo. As a result, the PLA focused on developing a coercive air campaign strategy, much like the one that occurred in Kosovo, along with the development of ascent, anti-satellite anti-ship ballistic missile systems in order to both compel and deter potential enemies.

Furthermore, in the wake of Operation Allied Force, the PLA continued to significantly increase its allocation of fiscal resources toward its modernization efforts. This has resulted in the PLA becoming the highest funded military force within the Asian region. However, much like the two previous cases, there appears to have been no discussion of casualty avoidance characteristic within the PLA throughout this period.

As Table 4 below indicates, the PLA exhibited four out of the five characteristics associated with a Western style of warfare in the wake of U.S. and NATO military action against the FRY in 1999. Therefore PLA attitudes and approaches toward warfare have continued to trend toward becoming more Western.

Table 4. Manifestation of Western Characteristics of Warfare and
Post-U.S./NATO Operations against FRY

WESTERN CHARACTERISTICS OF WARFARE	CASE STUDIES
	2000-Today
	PLA Actions/Developments Post-U.S./NATO Intervention in Kosovo
Emphasis Placed on Technology	Yes
Emphasis on Discipline and Training	Yes
Exhibited Willingness to Change/Learn	Yes
Allocation of Economic Resources in Support of Modernization	Yes
Casualty Aversion	No

Source: Created by author.

PLA Westernization and the Regional Balance of Power

If Chinese military modernization efforts continue at their current pace, then the PLA will likely improve its capabilities over time. The PLA will be able to comprehensively defend the Chinese homeland and coastline beyond the "First Island Chain," a line that runs north-south roughly from the Kurile Islands, through the Japanese and Ryukyu Islands, to Taiwan and the Philippines, and further into the Pacific region. The gap between compelling and deterring capabilities vis-à-vis Taiwan will close significantly and the PLA will likely be able to deny U.S. naval and air access to the region possibly out to the "Second Island Chain" area past the Philippine Islands and toward Guam.[153]

Additionally, if China's ground force capabilities increase in conjunction with greater development of Chinese naval and airlift capabilities, China could possibly decide to use these force packages in a number of ways. For example, the PLA could be prepared to conduct regional and perhaps global non-combatant evacuation of Chinese citizens that are threatened, as

---

[153]U.S. DOD, *Annual Report to Congress: Military and Security Developments Involving the People's Republic of China 2013,* 34.

well as unilateral or partnered anti-piracy operations well beyond China's shores. Additionally, and if deemed necessary, the PLA could be capable of unilaterally securing key economic interests or sea lines of communication (SLOC) in the region, such as through the Strait of Malacca.[154]

However, most devastating to continued PLA Westernization efforts in the short term would be a direct and sustained confrontation with the U.S. (e.g., over Taiwanese sovereignty). This would surely exhaust a Chinese military in the relatively nascent stages of its military modernization efforts along Western-lines. PRC officials most likely realize this, hence their preference for limited and local wars that are relatively short.

Not relying solely on its hard power deterrence alone, China will use other elements of its national power (i.e., soft power) to target the third element of the Clausewitzian trinity; that being an adversary's population and its will.[155] Associated Chinese concepts such as "Three Warfares" with its psychological, media, and legal components must be considered when determining how China intends to conduct any operation tied to any possible security and foreign policy objectives discussed here.[156]

China's efforts to conduct humanitarian and disaster relief operations for its own citizens within China in time of need will improve and could possibly be called upon to further regional goodwill towards China if used accordingly. Though unlikely, China may possibly decide to take

---

[154]Mehmood-Ul-Hassan Khan, "China's First Aircraft Carrier: A Research Study," *Defence Journal* 15, no. 1/2 (2011): 53-62.

[155]Carl von Clausewitz, Michael Howard, and Peter Paret, *On War,* eds. Michael Howard and Peter Paret (Princeton, NJ: Princeton University Press, 1984), 78; and Joseph S. Nye, *The Future of Power*, 1st ed. (New York, NY: Public Affairs, 2011), 19-24.

[156]Dennis J. Blasko, *The Chinese Army Today : Tradition and Transformation for the 21st Century* (New York, NY: Routledge, 2006), 164; David Shambaugh, "China Flexes Its Soft Power," *The New York Times,* 7 June 2010; and Wortzel, 151-162.

the lead in some international humanitarian and disaster relief efforts in order to increase its regional influence.

That said, the increasing Westernization of the PLA is not occurring in a vacuum, and Beijing's ability to shift the regional balance of military power must take into consideration a number of factors. First, barring any unforeseen shift or change in U.S. security commitment to the region (c.f., 1969 Nixon "Guam" doctrine), the Asian region will most likely continue to have a persistent U.S. presence due to the security and economic interests involving the U.S. and its allies and partners.

Second, other regional powers such as India, Russia, and Japan, as well as Taiwan and South Korea, will most likely not sit idle in their own respective military development and modernization efforts. As China's military capabilities increase, so will the militaries of other regional powers.

Third, continued heavy investment and budget allocation toward defense spending by the PRC is highly dependent upon continued economic growth of the Chinese economy. Possible economic shocks or downturns may cause China's leaders to make necessary budgetary compromises similar to those made in the early 1980s in order to focus on other domestic priorities.

Lastly, Chinese military modernization may still be hampered by its defense industry and the "firewall" that separates its civilian and defense sectors.[157] This limits the PLA's ability to make weapons procurement and development decisions solely based on sound military practicality, as opposed to other less militarily relevant interests, such as those tied to state owned business interests. Furthermore, while China remains dependent upon foreign technology from such suppliers as Russia, it is uncertain how long countries like Russia would be willing to

---

[157]Shambaugh, *Modernizing China's Military: Progress, Problems, and Prospects*, 240 .

continue such transfers of technology if they began to perceive China as a threat to their own security.

Nevertheless, China does have money and time on its side. If the PRC can maintain the relatively stable environment it has enjoyed for approximately the last 20 years, continue to benefit from its economic growth, and continue to ameliorate most of its deficient areas, then the PLA will likely be able to continue to develop those naval, air, and land forces that will afford it comprehensive military capabilities commensurate with its great power goals.

CONCLUSION

This monograph has argued that three events in particular—the 1979 Sino-Vietnamese conflict, the 1991 U.S. Gulf War, and U.S. and NATO military action against the FRY in 1999— have contributed to a consistent PLA movement toward greater Westernization in its approaches toward and preparations for war. The abysmal performance of the PLA during the 1979 Sino-Vietnamese conflict marked the nadir for the Maoist operating concept of people's war, and served as a point of departure toward greater military Westernization. Additionally, both the 1991 Gulf War, and U.S. and NATO military action in Kosovo served to reinforce the trend in modern Chinese military development toward greater Westernization.

Finally, as table 5 summarizes below, PLA attitudes and approaches toward warfare from 1979 to today have trended toward becoming more Western. Four out of the five characteristics of a Western form of warfare have manifested themselves throughout the three chosen case studies. However, the fifth—casualty aversion—does not appear to be a current feature of PLA approaches to warfighting. Additionally, future research would benefit the ongoing analysis of China's military development by exploring the possible military advantages associated with an increasingly Westernized PLA that also possesses a relatively higher tolerance for casualties in relation to any future adversary.

50

Table 5. Western Characteristics of Warfare across Three Case Studies

WESTERN CHARACTERISTICS OF WARFARE	CASE STUDIES		
	1979-1990	1991-1998	2000-Today
	PLA Actions/Developments Post-Sino-Vietnamese Conflict	PLA Actions/Developments Post-U.S. Gulf War	PLA Actions/Developments Post-U.S./NATO Intervention in Kosovo
Emphasis Placed on Technology	Yes	Yes	Yes
Emphasis on Discipline and Training	Yes	Yes	Yes
Exhibited Willingness to Change/Learn/Adapt	Yes	Yes	Yes
Allocation of Fiscal Resources in Support of Modernization	No	Yes	Yes
Casualty Aversion	No	No	No

Source: Created by author.

BIBLIOGRAPHY

Blasko, Dennis J. *The Chinese Army Today : Tradition and Transformation for the 21st Century* New York, NY: Routledge, 2006.

_____. *Chinese Army Today: Tradition and Transformation for the 21st Century.* New York, NY: Routledge, 2012.

Citino, Robert Michael. *Blitzkrieg to Desert Storm: The Evolution of Operational Warfare.* Lawrence, KS: University Press of Kansas, 2004.

Deng, Xiaoping. "Speech at an Enlarged Meeting of the Military Commission of the Central Committee of the Communist Party of China." People's Daily Online, 4 June 1985. http://english.peopledaily.com.cn/dengxp/vol3/text/c1410.html (accessed 5 February 2014).

Deng, Xiaoping and Zhongguo gong chan dang. Zhong yang Makesi En'gesi Liening Sidalin zhu zuo bian yi ju. *Selected Works of Deng Xiaoping, 1982-1992.* Vol. 3. 1st ed. Beijing, China: Foreign Language Press, 1994.

Dreyer, June Teufel. *The PLA and the Kosovo Conflict.* Carlisle Barracks, PA: Strategic Studies Institute, U.S. Army War College, 2000.

The Editorial Board. "China's Evolving 'Core Interests'," *The New York Times*, 11 May 2013. http://www.nytimes.com/2013/05/12/opinion/sunday/chinas-evolving-core-interests.html?_r=0 (accessed 22 February 2014).

Godwin, Paul H.B. "Compensating for Deficiencies: Doctrinal Evolution in the Chinese People's Liberation Army 1978-1999." In *Seeking Truth from Facts : A Retrospective on Chinese Military Studies in the Post-Mao Era.* Edited by James C. Mulvenon and Andrew N.D. Yang, 213. Santa Monica, CA: National Security Research Division, RAND, 2001.

Hanson, Victor Davis. *The Western Way of War: Infantry Battle in Classical Greece.* 1st ed. New York, NY: Knopf, 1989.

Hawkins, Charles F. "The People's Liberation Army Looks to the Future." *JFQ: Joint Force Quarterly*, no. 25 (2000): 12-16.

Heath, Timothy. "Restructuring the Military: Drivers and Prospects for Xi's Top-Down Reforms." The Jamestown Foundation. http://www.jamestown.org/programs/chinabrief/single/?tx_ttnews%5Btt_news%5D=41936&tx_ttnews%5BbackPid%5D=25&cHash=12cb9c60b4b918bb7d80cfef503069d1 - .UwpwuHm3T4g (accessed 22 February 2014).

Hsu, Immanuel C.Y. *The Rise of Modern China.* 6th ed. New York, NY: Oxford University Press, 2000.

Huaqing, Liu. "Unswervingly Advance Along the Road of Building a Modern Army with Chinese Characteristics." *Jiefangjun Bao,* 18 August 1993. Foreign Broadcast Information Service.

Human Rights Watch. "China: Human Rights Concerns in Xinjiang." Human Rights Watch, October 2001. http://www.hrw.org/reports/2001/10/18/china-human-rights-concerns-xinjiang (accessed 22 February 2014).

Information Office of the State Council, The People's Republic of China. "China's National Defense." China.org.cn, July 1998. http://www.china.org.cn/e-white/5/index.htm (accessed 5 February 2014).

_____. "China's National Defense in 2010." Xinuanet, 31 March 2011. http://news.xinhuanet.com/english2010/china/2011-03/31/c_13806851.htm (accessed 12 November 2013).

_____. "The Diversified Employment of China's Armed Forces." Xinhuanet, 16 April 2013. http://news.xinhuanet.com/english/china/2013-04/16/c_132312681.htm (accessed 13 November 2013).

Institute for Strategic Studies. *The Military Balance*. London, England: Institute for Strategic Studies, 1991.

_____. *The Military Balance*. London, England: Institute for Strategic Studies, 1992.

_____. *The Military Balance*. London, England: Institute for Strategic Studies, 1995.

_____. *The Military Balance*. London, England: Institute for Strategic Studies, 2001.

Joffe, Ellis. *The Chinese Army after Mao*. Cambridge, MA: Harvard University Press, 1987.

Kamphausen, Roy, David Lai and Andrew Scobell. *The PLA at Home and Abroad :Assessing the Operational Capabilities of China's Military*. Edited by Roy Kamphausen, David Lai and Andrew Scobell. Carlisle, PA: Strategic Studies Institute, U.S. Army War College, 2010.

Khan, Mehmood-Ul-Hassan. "China's First Aircraft Carrier: A Research Study." *Defence Journal* 15, no. 1/2 (2011): 53-62.

Lauren, Paul Gordon, Gordon Alexander Craig and Alexander L. George. *Force and Statecraft : Diplomatic Challenges of Our Time*. 4th ed. New York, NY: Oxford University Press, 2007.

Liberation Army Daily. Quoted in Gerald Segal. *Defending China*. Oxford, NY: Oxford University Press, 1985.

Luttwak, Edward N. "Toward Post-Heroic Warfare." *Foreign Affairs* 74, no. 3 (1995): 109-122.

McNeal, Dewardic L. Congressional Research Service Report for Congress, *China's Relations with Central Asian States and Problems of Terrorism*. Policy Archive, 17 December 2001. http://research.policyarchive.org/1315.pdf (accessed 22 February 2014).

Mulvenon, James C. and Andrew N.D. Yang, eds. *Seeking Truth from Facts : A Retrospective on Chinese Military Studies in the Post-Mao Era*. Santa Monica, CA: National Security Research Division, RAND, 2001.

Mulvenon, James C. and David Michael Finkelstein. *China's Revolution in Doctrinal Affairs Emerging Trends in the Operational Art of the Chinese People's Liberation Army.* CNA Corporation, 2005. http://www.cna.org/documents/DoctrineBook.pdf (accessed 5 February 2014).

Murphey, Rhoads. *East Asia: A New History.* 5th ed. Boston, MA: Longman, 2010.

Newmyer, Jacqueline. "The Revolution in Military Affairs with Chinese Characteristics." *Journal of Strategic Studies* 33, no. 4 (2010): 483-504.

Noonan, Michael P. "The Illusion of Bloodless Victories." *Orbis* 41, no. 2 (1997): 308-319.

Nye, Joseph S. *The Future of Power.* 1st ed. New York, NY: Public Affairs, 2011.

Paret, Peter. *The Cognitive Challenge of War: Prussia 1806.* Princeton, NJ: Princeton University Press, 2009.

Parker, Geoffrey. *The Cambridge Illustrated History of Warfare: The Triumph of the West.* Rev. and updated ed. Cambridge , NY: Cambridge University Press, 2008.

Pillsbury, Michael. *Chinese Views of Future Warfare.* Edited by Michael Pillsbury. Washington, DC: National Defense University Press, 1998.

Ryan, Mark A., David Michael Finkelstein and Michael A. McDevitt. *Chinese Warfighting: The PLA Experience since 1949.* Armonk, NY: M.E. Sharpe, 2003.

Secretary of Defense and Chairman of the Joint Chiefs of Staff. Report to Congress, *Operation Allied Force: After-Action Report.* U.S. Department of Defense, 31 January 2000. http://www.dod.mil/pubs/kaar02072000.pdf (accessed 22 February 2014).

Segal, Gerald. *Defending China.* Oxford, NY: Oxford University Press, 1985.

Shambaugh, David. "China Flexes Its Soft Power." *The New York Times,* 7 June 2010.

_____. *Modernizing China's Military: Progress, Problems, and Prospects.* Berkeley, CA: University of California Press, 2002.

Shirk, Susan L. *China: Fragile Superpower.* Oxford, NY: Oxford University Press, 2007.

Swaine, Michael D. "China's Assertive Behavior—Part One: On 'Core Interests'." *China Leadership Monitor,* no. 34 (2011): 1-25. http://www.hoover.org/publications/china-leadership-monitor (accessed 22 February 2014).

Thomas, Timothy L. *Decoding the Virtual Dragon.* Fort Leavenworth, KS: Foreign Military Studies Office, 2007.

_____. *Dragon Bytes : Chinese Information-War Theory and Practice from 1995-2003.* Fort Leavenworth, KS: Foreign Military Studies Office, 2004.

U.S. Department of Defense. *Annual Report to Congress: Military Power of the People's Republic of China 2006.* U.S. Department of Defense, 2006. http://www.defense.gov/pubs/pdfs/China%20Report%202006.pdf (accessed 22 February 2014).

———. *Annual Report to Congress: Military Power of the People's Republic of China 2007.* U.S. Department of Defense, 2007. http://www.defense.gov/pubs/pdfs/070523-China-Military-Power-final.pdf (accessed 22 February 2014).

———. *Annual Report to Congress: Military Power of the People's Republic of China 2008.* U.S. Department of Defense, 2008. http://www.defense.gov/pubs/pdfs/China_Military_Report_08.pdf (accessed 22 February 2014).

———. *Annual Report to Congress: Military Power of the People's Republic of China 2009.* U.S. Department of Defense, 2009. http://www.defense.gov/pubs/pdfs/china_military_power_report_2009.pdf (accessed 22 February 2014).

———. *Annual Report to Congress: Military and Security Developments Involving the People's Republic of China 2010.* U.S. Department of Defense, 2010. http://www.defense.gov/pubs/pdfs/2010_cmpr_final.pdf (accessed 22 February 2014).

———. *Annual Report to Congress: Military and Security Developments Involving the People's Republic of China 2011.* U.S. Department of Defense, 2011. http://www.defense.gov/pubs/pdfs/2011_cmpr_final.pdf (accessed 22 February 2014).

———. *Annual Report to Congress: Military and Security Developments Involving the People's Republic of China 2013.* U.S. Department of Defense, 2013. http://www.defense.gov/pubs/2013_china_report_final.pdf (accessed 22 February 2014).

———. *FY04 Report to Congress on PRC Military Power Pursuant to the FY2000 National Defense Authorization Act, Annual Report on the Military Power of the People's Republic of China.* U.S. Department of Defense, 2004. http://www.defense.gov/pubs/d20040528PRC.pdf (accessed 22 February 2014).

———. *Report to Congress Pursuant to the FY2000 National Defense Authorization Act, Annual Report on the Military Power of the People's Republic of China.* U.S. Department of Defense, 2002. http://www.defense.gov/news/Jul2002/d20020712china.pdf (accessed 22 February 2014).

von Clausewitz, Carl. *On War.* Translated by Michael Howard and Peter Paret. Princeton, NJ: Princeton University Press, 1984.

The World Bank. "Data: GDP Growth (Annual %)." The World Bank Group. http://data.worldbank.org/country/china (accessed 9 March 2014).

Wortzel, Larry M. *The Dragon Extends Its Reach: Chinese Military Power Goes Global.* 1st ed. Sterling, VA: Potomac Books, 2013.

Wu, Jiao and Xiao Hui. "Modern Limited War Calls for Reform of Traditional Military Principles." *Guofang Daxue Xuebao* (November 1987). Quoted in *Seeking Truth from Facts : A Retrospective on Chinese Military Studies in the Post-Mao Era* , 98. Edited by

James C. Mulvenon and Andrew N.D. Yang. Santa Monica, CA: National Security Research Division, RAND, 2001.

Xiong, Guangkai. *Guo Ji Zhan LüE Yu Xin Jun Shi Bian Ge - International Strategy and Revolution in Military Affairs*. Di 1 ban. ed. Beijing, China: Qing hua da xue chu ban she, 2003.

Zedong, Mao. *Selected Military Writings of Mao Tse-Tung*. Edited by Combat Studies Institute. Fort Leavenworth, KS: U.S. Army Command and General Staff College, 2012.